D1117773

Everything I Need to Know I Learned From LED ZEPPELIN

The Enthusiast publishes books and paper goods. Subjects include, vintage how-to, retro-cooking and home economics, holidays and celebrations, games and puzzles, graphic design, classic children's literature, illustrated literature and poetry, humour.

What's Your Passion?

 Enthusiast.cc

✉ TheEnthusiast@Enthusiast.cc

ISBN / EAN

EBook Edition   1595837477 / 9781595837479
Standard Edition 1595837485 / 9781595837486

When I was sixteen years old my best friend, Paul, and I built a "Super Stereo." An elaborate contraption involving multiple stero amplifiers and four, nearly-tall-as-a-man, speakers that Paul had built in his Dad's garage. One day after school, all the adults being at work, we played *Whole Lotta Love* so loud that the windows in my California tract home actually rattled. The neighbors called the cops, and the Super Stereo was sadly never heard from again. Over the ensuing years Led Zeppelin and their wonderful music and lyrics have continued to inspire and instruct me. From too numerous to be counted impromptu sing-alongs in cars and living rooms, to an elaborately choreographed version of *Fool In the Rain* that still begs to be turned into a full fledged opera; it would seem that my creativity and 'getting the Led out' remain inextricably and inexplicably intertwined. *Everything I Need to Know I Learned From Led Zeppelin* is a combination of my love for Led Zeppelin and my collection of vintage children's readers and school primers, mostly from the era of my childhood. The lyrics presented are those that, for me at least, fit so beautifully with the artwork. They are positive, inspirational and philosophical, as is much of Led Zeppelin's work. The aptness of the combinations, like a lot delightful, things, defies easy explanation. I can only mildly suggest that the Dick-and-Jane like pictures and the Led Zeppelin lyrics both live in timeless, inevitable, spaces, like Elvis Presley movies, the Eiffel Tower, and Buster Keaton, and so just naturally go well together.

- Benjamin Darling

Sing loud for the sunshine, pray hard for the rain.

And show your love for Lady Nature.

I'm telling you now,
The greatest thing
you ever can do now, is
trade a smile with
someone who's blue
now, It's very easy.

So anytime somebody needs you, don't let them down, although it grieves you.

If you feel that you can't go on and your will's sinking low, just believe and you can't go wrong. In the light, you will find the road.

I am just a simple guy,
I live from day to day.
A ray of sunshine melts
my frown and blows my
blues away.

Many dreams come true and some have silver linings.

Mellow is the man who knows what he's been missing.

19

Many is a word that only leaves you guessing, Guessing 'bout a thing you really ought to know.

No use hiding in a corner,
Cause that won't change a thing.

25

Yes, there are two paths you can go by, but in the long run there's still time to change the road you're on.

27

In a tree by the brook,
there's a songbird who sings,
Sometimes all of our thoughts
are misgiven.

28

And it's whispered that soon, if we all call the tune, Then the piper will lead us to reason

This is the mystery of the quotient - Upon us all a little rain must fall

So tonight you better stop and rebuild all your ruins because peace and trust can win the day.

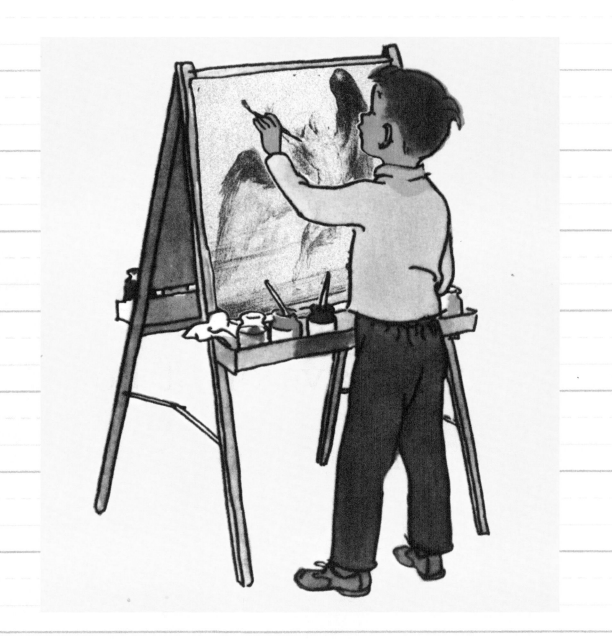

Oh let the sun beat down upon my face, stars to fill my dream I am a traveler of both time and space to be where I have been.

Sit and wait and all will be revealed.

Held now within the knowing. Rest now within the peace. Take of the fruit, but guard the seed.

And if you listen very hard, the tune will come to you at last.

47

When all is one and one is all, to be a rock and not to roll.

IF THERE'S A BUSTLE IN YOUR HEDGEROW, DON'T BE ALARMED NOW, IT'S JUST A SPRING CLEAN FOR THE MAY QUEEN.

THERE'S A SIGN ON THE WALL BUT SHE WANTS TO BE SURE 'CAUSE YOU KNOW SOMETIMES WORDS HAVE TWO MEANINGS.

Then as it was, then again it will be. Though the course may change sometimes, rivers always reach the sea.

Many times I've
wondered
How much there is to
know

It's lonely at the bottom, Man, it's dizzy at the top. But if you're standing in the middle, Ain't no way you're gonna stop.

If the sun refused to shine I would still be loving you. When mountains crumble to the sea there will still be you and me.

3 1333 04196 9880

CPSIA information can be obtained at www.ICGtesting.com
Printed in the USA
LVOW02s1542260214

375272LV00002B/4/P